Echoes from the Peaceable Kingdom

by
JOHN BENNETT

Foreword
by
CHAD WALSH

WILLIAM B. EERDMANS PUBLISHING COMPANY
Grand Rapids, Michigan

To Catherine and Jennifer
With Love for All the Days of Their Lives

Library of Congress Cataloging in Publication Data

Bennett, John Frederic.
    Echoes from the peaceable kingdom.

    Poems.
    1. Animals — Poetry. I. Title.
PS3552.E547E3   811'.5'4   78-1348
ISBN 0-8028-3510-4

For permission to reprint certain poems in this book, I wish to thank the editors
of The New York Times, The Chicago Daily News, Prairie Schooner, Wisconsin
Academy Review, St. Norbert College Press, and especially Sydon Press which published
an earlier version of the text in an abridged, limited edition entitled The Zoo Manuscript.

In addition, I wish to thank Mrs. Peggy Schlapman for her endless care in typing the
poems through revision after revision. But above all, I wish to thank my wife Elizabeth
and our daughters Catherine and Jennifer, who still insist upon taking me to the zoo.

FOREWORD

In a time when rising poets have discovered the art of public relations, and clamber up to public attention through the cultivation of newsworthy eccentricities, aided by an interlocking directorate of little magazines, news magazines, foundations, cliques, and poetry-reading tours, John Bennett has gone his quiet way, uninvolved in the politics of poetry, and little known to even the reasonably well-informed students of contemporary poetry. He has spent more time writing his poetry than promoting it.

Echoes from the Peaceable Kingdom reveals a great talent and a particular insight. Of the first, certain things are so evident they scarcely need to be said. There is an infallible ear at work here; rhythm and melody are uncannily exact, always just right for the particular poem, never forced or superimposed on the poem itself. The diction, while often breathtakingly novel, always has the same air of simple inevitability; it is the perfect complement of the substance and mood of each poem. Metaphor is unfailingly concrete and accurate. Rime itself seems to grow organically from some central life, rather than being a willed and additional ornament.

What I have written so far sounds like the praises one would bestow on any good poet. But there is a special inner quality here that is harder to analyze. What I see is a distinctively Celtic imagination at work, fed on the pre-Christian Irish poets, and deeply but subtly indebted to William Butler Yeats, the C. S. Lewis of the trilogy and Narnia stories, and J. R. R. Tolkien. It is a druidic sensibility that has undergone a profound Christian baptism along the way, but in the conversion of the outer and inner eyes nothing of its old natural magic has been lost.

The angle of vision is unique among contemporary

poets. There is the ability to look at the earth and its denizens with an eye both photographic and mythopoeic, and always loving; the tenderness, at once severe and brotherly, that sees some of Eden's dew on all creatures, but with double sight recognizes at all times that Eden has been lost and only its haunting memories remain, evoked in brief flashes when innocence still meets innocence —

> *Caught up in joy and April and surprise,*
> *sweet Jennifer becomes a magic where:*
> *surrounded by small creatures of her Lord,*
> *she brings the sun to glory in her hair,*
> *and the blue Celtic distance lights her eyes.*

Like the medieval bestiaries that are its distant model, *Echoes from the Peaceable Kingdom* presents a *jardin zoologique moralisé* in which

> *Nine rabbits, caged concupiscents, insist*
> *that procreation be a public act*

while

> *Close by, in suburbs bordering the zoo,*
> *the people act much as the rabbits do,*
> *and Malthus sleeps in his triumphant earth.*

If traces of Eden survive in the permanent inhabitants of the zoo, their distant or close cousins show in varied ways that for them Eden is a memory, not an abiding home:

> *The Primate House tolls other primates in*
> *who, having come to watch their alien kin,*
> *move oddly through some fear or cruelty*
> *that will not let their eyes see what they see.*

Man's unthinking and unfeeling alienation from his fellow creatures is repeatedly pictured, as in the concluding horror of the rhinoceros poem:

Within a bursting shade, green, hot, and full,
the bullets strike, a sinewed pattern fails,
the horns are savaged from the broken skull,
an ageless strength dissolves to stinking grue.

But the splendor of creation survives the malice of its fallen race. At times, the sheer wonder of shape and color inspires lines that have the bright precision of illuminations in a medieval manuscript:

the alligator sleeps amid a spill
of mossy turtles dyed algaic green.
Incredibly heraldic, it is set
gris, mailed, and couchant *on a field of wet.*

There is in these poems something of a St. Francis, standing in delight as he beholds the abundance and fantastic variety of life that the Creator has bestowed upon the world. Never falsely sentimental, never forgetting the chasms between man and beast, John Bennett sees them as creatures who have issued from the same divine hand. The opening poem invokes "Old Adam" who "stood/in human splendor once in Eden wood/and dreamed the holy names," and concludes with the prayer:

stand softly at the center of my skull
and chant your early metaphors of love
and set their joy against the bent world's rage.

The giraffe becomes the evidence of God's fantastic dreaming —

Of all the myriad that throngs the zoo,
it is,
            if unbelieved,
                        the creature who
can demonstrate for children what God sees

> as He dreams forth a world that is adorned
> (as April worlds should be) with gentleness —
> and magic worked beyond its last degrees.

And in the final poem, the act of creation is viewed not as a once-and-for-all deed of the distant past, but as a continuing outreach of the Creator's teeming love:

> Then here see water, flesh, and fire glance
> upon and through each other:
>   such acts praise
> a God who swims through all evolving worlds
> as He creates them out of death and night.
> The Paraclete sustains the otter dance
> and all the dances in the spheres of light.

I search in vain to find other contemporary poems like these. By evoking with heart's love and mind's skill a vision as old as St. Francis' and older, John Bennett has given us poetry more modern than modern. *Echoes from the Peaceable Kingdom* is *sui generis* and it is here to stay.

Chad Walsh
Beloit College

CONTENTS

Echoes from the Peaceable Kingdom

1

Old Adam, father, poet, priest, you stood
in human splendor once in Eden wood
and dreamed the holy names; your dreaming spoke
the beasts alive with that first poetry.

So now, Old Father, stranger to an age
when poems are thin knives or bitter smoke,
stand softly at the center of my skull
and chant your early metaphors of love
and set their joy against the bent world's rage.

2

Caught up in joy and April and surprise,
sweet Jennifer becomes a magic where:
surrounded by small creatures of her Lord,
she brings the sun to glory in her hair,
and the blue Celtic distance lights her eyes.

Bemused and happy in the Children's Zoo,
she meets with love that can be purely met
amid the gentle seekings young things do:
child, fawn, kid, lamb and tiny leveret
define a force poor Huxley never knew.

3

The zoo/aquarium displays
the patterns of repeated ways.
Brought here to magic square or round,
the mythic prototypes abound:
the narwhal with its spiral horn
contains the shining unicorn;
the griffin hides its eagle claw
within the lion's dreaming paw;
the dugongs once and anciently
gave birth to mermaids in the sea;
the great komodo lizards keep
dragons within them, fast asleep;
the old camelopards come down
from distant tapestries to merge
with young giraffes in Masai brown.
The zoo is built on Plato's verge:
it lives in Plato's honeyed head.

4

Like missionary priests from some bland creed,
the sacerdotal penguins veer and stomp
on wet rocks altarwise into a spray
from rusty pipes that emphasize their pomp:
erect and fat and feathered all the way,
they lean whenever gravity shows need,
yet somehow they maintain a level sway.

In quick reversal, then, they turn and dive
into the mimic, clear, Antarctic sea
held up around the rocks by crystal glass
which, locked in space, lets doubtful humans see
that birds (or eerie more-than-birds) can pass
from sphere to deeper sphere; that they can flee
beyond dead levels of expectancy,
beyond the stupid anarchies of fact.

The penguins swim batlike through undersea:
outside the zoo, in flowing, wider lives,
the loon or grebe or water ouzel dives
through parallels to penguins joyously.

5

Broader than boats, deeper than trout brooks are,
the hippo turns submersible at will,
or then bobs up like fatly muscled cork
that heaves his cloudy pond to overspill.

Earthshaking river-creature, miracle
of piggy flesh and long aquatic skill,
his tonnage is the pure amphibious,
not bound like some to fluke and spiracle.

Snoutdeep in hyacinths or deeper yet,
the hippo once possessed the Nile as home:
he was a Grecian joke; or he was Set;
he stood as solid as the church at Rome,
or rolled, transported, through disportive wet,
godlike and fat in hyacinthine foam.

6

Though closely lodged in paddock, hutch, or pen,
all creatures are their archetypic selves,
and they remain so, whether caged or free:

the stoutest digger found in field or fen,
old truepenny that covers moles with shame,
old pioner, old earthsplitter that delves
under the greensward, under the rock and tree,
the badger is the badger endlessly,
wholly himself, claw, flesh, and form, and name.

Mustelic, grey, and fiercely obdurate,
he simply sits upon the stony floor
which yields no meaning to his digger's claws
or, watching sticks small boys thrust at his door,
walks backward from offenses that are small
or moves against them when they grow too great.

He is unlike his neighbor, a young skunk
(but also kin) that frets on aimless paws
and wanders back and forth from wall to wall.

7

Old dragon form *sans* wing and firelung,
and medieval as a corkindrill,
the alligator sleeps amid a spill
of mossy turtles dyed algaic green.
Incredibly heraldic, it is set
gris, mailed, and *couchant* on a field of wet.

It moves.
        A flare of basilisk leaps out
from vitric eye, from slowly yawning snout.

8

Albino, Flemish, and Chinchilla, mixed,
nine rabbits flow through poses never fixed.

Nine rabbits, caged concupiscents, insist
that procreation be a public act.
Though wilder rabbits dance by moonlight, these
dismay the orthodox with noonday ease.

Their bland and furry lechings can distract
a casual eye.
                        Within such lively dust,
a cosmic force devolves to hopping lust:
that force, so changed, gives little rise to mirth.
Close by, in suburbs bordering the zoo,
the people act much as the rabbits do,
and Malthus sleeps in his triumphant earth.

Nine rabbits move through poses never fixed,
Albino, Flemish, and Chinchilla, mixed.

9

Through horizontal depths of air
wild birds fall parallel to earth.
The latest robin leaves the sky
to learn circumference of green:
it merges maple into self
and unifies the April scene.

That unity invites the eye:
circumference of leaf and bird
spreads outward from the varied zoo
to meet the round and rush of sky.

10

The cockroach, racial conqueror of time
(except in Polar Zones) can die of fear,
it is so finely made.
                                Nevertheless,
it prospers calmly in a seething clime,
surrounded by huge forms of mouse and deer,
of wallaby and ape and lioness.

Shy, brown, and social only with its kind,
it will not, settled in, desert this state:
it is too hungry, quick, and delicate —
and has, besides, a wholly changeless mind.

11

(For Catherine)

Though unicorn and griffin now are lost
to human dream, the elephant remains:
the roots of heaven, metaphoric, strong,
strike down through western zoos and eastern plains.

Once fief to Prester John, the great gray beast
accepts a gesture from a frolic child
who gives an echo of God's glee to know
that massive strength and gentleness can grow
together in a form so huge, so mild.

The chemic arrogance which hopes to build
its cobbling of God's joy should try this move:
an elephant, met by a little girl
who races toward him over April lawns
and touches him with hands that offer love.

12

As dulcet-eyed as ever Io was,
the yak, Tibetan, dark, and of a size
so gentle that she overwhelms surmise,
comes pacing softly to her wire fence
and thrusts against it with her dainty nose.

Pity poor Zeus, who knew a lovely wench,
and Hera, hurt by protophallic sin,
who could not wander into eastern snows
nor dream this shape to cast sweet heifers in.

13

Some randy motion in the Spring
can hurl the dullest bird a-wing,
or catch the tortoise up in glee
engendering new progeny.

On three-toed feet, the cassowary bobs
across a dingy lawn;
                           its feathers hang
like tendrils from a shape ovoid and high;
it turns its head and blinks a lizard eye
against the sun;
                           its crest and wattles gleam
with April light;
                           emu and ostrich seem
mere shadows from some cassowary dream.

On that same grass, a dreaming tortoise shares
the lettuce, carrots, bread, and such bland tares
as keepers of the zoo think they should yield
to flightless creatures in a narrow field.

Some randy motion in the Spring
can hurl the dullest bird a-wing
and catch the tortoise up in glee
engendering new progeny.

14

Beneath the lively zoo, the somewhere bones
of megatherium lie sprawled and still,
an odd concatenation of queer stones
whose modern child, the sloth, hangs upside down
in catatonic green that's not its own.

Moved turgidly through atavistic will,
two-toed or three, the sloth is stiffly made
to hang upon a stiffened bough and keep
itself dissolved in dullness and green shade.

To sleep so much makes murder out of sleep.
What made the fungus quit its searching drive
and trust itself to upside-down and hair?
What made the sloth desert the quickened earth
and marry slowness on a leafy stair?

15

The Primate House tolls other primates in
who, having come to watch their alien kin,
move oddly through some fear or cruelty
that will not let their eyes see what they see.

Orangutan, his reddish beard awry,
sleeps on a swaying plank in middle air,
but such a bed, so flat and smooth and bare,
could never slant from a Sumatran tree.
Illusion breaks with sleep. His fingers clench,
his ancient eyes grow wide, he moves a knee —
and then relaxes to a long despair
like some old hobo on a public bench.

The gibbon cannot brachiate between
such rigid trees as iron bars devise:
he does gymnastics through his narrow scene
and seeks a springy bough where no boughs rise.
A young girl watches him. Her innocence
mistakes his boredom for exuberance.

Locked firmly in by walls of armor glass,
the shy gorilla tries to hide among
the angled lights where shadows always die,
where days, too much illumined, merely pass.
The Tanganyikan succulence that gave
sweet roots to mountain slopes and pleased his tongue;
the jungle growth that was a springing cave,
a world of green-gold joy that fed his joy
and kept it safe from any greedy eye; —

all these are lost, paid out to buy a pen
that's never closed against the stares of men.

'Four hundred eighty pounds,' so says the sign,
'and not full grown.' Two hundred more will make
a proper ape of him so he can twist
old tires into pretzels, play the fool,
climb bars to please a crowd of gawps, and shake
the heavy glass with battered foot and fist.

The Primate House tolls other primates in
who, having come to watch their alien kin,
move oddly through some fear or cruelty
that will not let their eyes see what they see.

16

A melanistic prize, a rarity
as sinuous as wind or waterflow,
the leopard wears its fiery blackness tight
against a shape ripped from the flesh of night.

It paces deep behind the slender bars;
its eyes flame outward, fierce as feral stars,
to mark a self-transcendence;
                              their green glow
contains the voids that Blake imagined, once,
to name the Tyger's birth, the world's dark woe.

And Hemingway has carved a myth in prose
to prove that leopards lunge beyond the world:
on Kilimanjaro, high above the plains
where Eden could resume, a leopard found
peculiar death amid the mortal snows,
but left its flesh to frighten and confound
the baffled wanderers who found it there,
a ghost dissolving into withered air,
a force becoming its eternity,
a leopard dead where leopards could not be.

17

One crazy anger troubles all the scene.

Brought down from Northern wilds, the wolverine
is more mephitic than his smaller kin
or more devoted to a rage within.

He crouches round that rage and snaps his jaws,
his eyes glare red, he lurches at the brink
of always murder on his scrabbling paws.

The otter moves through grace; the weasel moves
at least through graceful speed; even the skunk
moves through placidity:
                                        the wolverine
moves only, endlessly, through snarl and stink.

He is the maddest creature in the scene.

18

The zoo contains a paragon of sheep
more dignified than Ashur at his best,
and better bearded from his chin to chest,
that is, from jaw to brisket, down and down;

his horns re-entrant, carved from basalt, sweep
the coiling air;
                serene, tightskinned, and brown,
he stands unmoving where mere goats would dance
upon the edges of a rocky steep:

not Assurbanipal in his hot prime
(that ramping king follicular whose zest
could eat a world) had such a beard or crown.

The aoudad maintains a Grecian stance
and somehow lives in space but not in time.

19

The Reptile House is always still with death:

among dry grasses curled through glassy heat,
the prairie rattler lies, coiled tight and neat;
the great green mamba hangs upon a tree
that seems a poisoned thing, eternally;
fat sausage snake, the tommygoff lies bunched
as if in flowered bushcrown, shoulder high,
ready to sink its deadly cocksnout in
some jungle innocence that passes by;
even the smallest garter snake glides through
a gelid rite, a grim significance,
a subtle winding into circumstance.

Lethal or not, these squamous creatures prove
that Emily was apt, her zero true,
while Coleridge was wrong: the worlds of love
lie far and far from here.
                  A cautious few
walk through the doorways on a shaky breath,
observe the Gaboon vipers, and then go
back into sunlight with a crippled glance
at that slim horror called the fer-de-lance:

the Reptile House is always still with death.

20

Within the pool that moats the Monkey Caves,
five black sea lions, magnified of seal,
flash underwater, round and round and round.

Swift-sounding wonders of aquatic force,
they race like submarines or, arching, leap
in dazzles up to gain a concrete wall.

And there sometimes they sleep, truly as if
grey western seawalls rose around the pool
whose neighbor pool is filled with golden carp.

21

Bred somehow in the zoo lagoon
where carp swim golden through wet shade,
the water skipper's purely made
of insect buoyancy. He leaps
past subtle tides that race around
those flimsy tensions in his floor
which keep him upright and undrowned.

He is both boat and acrobat:
with suddenly a casual ease
he darts on mimic voyages
across reflected skies and trees

and water warps beneath his weight
and each small insect foot reweaves
the image of a flindered bough
and its brief multitude of leaves

while he in minor triumph runs
upon a thin security
until he finds a proper place
to stand afloat where suns might see.

22

Some creatures moved unheeded through the zoo:
an ant, frenetic in the noonday sun,
defies the fiery light, the callous foot,
and charts the asphalt walk with nervous run
that leads to zigzag somewhere, to grass root —
cool chartreuse heaven on the other side —
or to some casual banquet rich and free
which it will carry/tumble/drag/or slide
down to the nest where fecund majesty,
blinded and helpless in a somber room,
compels its entry from the sunny world
into the tribal, regimented gloom.

23

In *cap-a-pie'* no soldier hopes to wear,
curled basketlike upon a silent shelf,
the armadillo, primitive and shy,
here keeps a second cage, its folded self.

Beyond that double cage, the pangolin,
the dragon mammal with its plated hide,
lies curled around its concentricity
and sleeps within itself, curved side by side.

With anteater and binturong, these two
bring Lewis Carroll straight into the zoo
and prove the joys of eccentricity,
a thing that goats and lions fail to do.

24

As agile-fingered as a capuchin,
maskfaced, ringtailed, brightly inquisitive,
bearlike in minor mimicry, and kin
to those great pandas Asiatics hoard,
the young raccoon sits on a weathered board
where all things else are wire or concrete
and eats a crust that water has made sweet.

Mewed up from bawling hounds, from warlike men
who lace the long autumnal nights with fear,
who shake the woods and crack a small heart's rhyme,
the young raccoon sits placid in her pen,
grown happy in accustomed innocence.

She lives securely caged against the time
when dogs and men seek ritual violence.

25

Chuckling and chortling, bright the mallards come
into the zoo. Their rapid slender wings,
which lately brought them from a warmer home,
brake back and up, and down they flare onto
the goose pools which they sometimes use instead
of crystal rivers or the green marshland
where vibrate reeds and singing cat-tails stand.
Lured down by power, corn, and week-old bread,
all drakes and susies know the world is free.

Meanwhile, like squadded Mandarins, the geese,
the pure conservators of all they see,
rise high upon their pools like angry fleece
and break the air with their resounding dree:

when wilderness comes, its quick quick joys upset
the ordered pools and make pomposity
a merest gooseflesh, raucous, mad, and wet.

26

But there are those that wander through the zoo
without intent, without a joyous mind.
Some humans measure so:

> one man guffaws,

slaps his broad ass, and burbles an applause
to see the baboon's rainbow of behind.

Well, all God's creatures prove a common plot
but these prove kissing cousins on the spot.

27

(For Douglas)

Bossed like Jove's front before his daughter came
to breach the godly bone, a massive head
swings placidly through stipples of green shade.

Much like a herdcock bull that's amply made
(virile, redundant, almost overbred,
eugenic, tested, sometimes almost tame),
the great Cape buffalo moves toward his shed.
His curving scimitars flash forth grey flame,
slight flies ride out the shrugging of his paunch,
the roof slants low above his armored head,
the doorposts gleam from rubbings by his haunch.

In him reflected see the Second Sign,
Europa riding whiteness in the sea,
the bulls for whom the slim-gut Cretans danced,
young Ariadne and her ball of twine
that taught a Greek to find the Minotaur,
the pure white bison from whom arrows glanced,
the water buffalo, the Indian gaur —
all real, all mythic masculinity.

28

The woodchuck, hoary earth-dweller of yore,
has now forgotten stonewalled clover or
his whistling need to dive beneath the farm.

Me imperturbe of animals at ease,
the wisest marmot in the rodent clan,
he watches motley crowds that slide and swarm
across his April day.
                        Content to please
or not to please, he has a Buddhic charm,
a furry grace, a somnolent *élan*.

29

The dolphin does not need to talk: it swims
with slamming verve through water merely wet
or hurls its quickblood body up through air
in curves of grace that graph a fish's flair.

But since some need for talking has been set
by men who backward yearn for saltiness,
the dolphin has been asked, from purest love,
to lend itself to verbal synergy
and add a footnote to semantic stress.

Ah! Cousteau and the dolphin surely prove
that going back to gills is hard, *pardee*!
or that the deepest knowledge we can wrest
from ichthygraph or *sprach-atlas,* at best,
is (vaguely) that men drown beneath the sea.

30

An architect of quick
on wings of shaking gauze,
a dragonfly whirls past
the fish and turtle pounds.

Small raptor of the zoo,
it hunts without a pause
through glints of silver-blue
above enormous grounds,

then hovers in its flight
above a dreaming fly:
from whorls of singing light
it stoops — or passes by.

31

Above the folds where deer and zebra keep
with peafowl and an intersperse of sheep,
redbodied swallows chart the April sky
on jewelled wings that gleam ecstatic glass.

Brief birdforms fall through curves that dip and pass
within the blink and instant of an eye:
among the shifting frontiers of soft blue,
the swallows dance above the heavy zoo.

32

The baffled polar bear plods down
cemented slopes to tepid water,
seeking a cleanly coldness which
was surely his in Arctic weathers.

He shakes his thrusting heavy head
against an arrogance of sun
and grunts that cold cannot be dead.
His white fur glints like egret feathers.

33

Some starlings, feathered cockroaches, drop free
from squirring flight into the maple tree
above the Lion House.
                              A great cat's roar
(ripped velvet changing into sonic glare)
hurls them aloft from their shrill tedium.

Among the swaying boughs, the shaken air
quickly regains its equilibrium.

34

Small refugees from roads now tarred and dead,
the sparrows sing bird praises in the dust
where bison shake the ground with heavy tread.

Sequestered from the hydrocarbon voids,
they also praise goats, antelope, and deer.
An engined world is one they cannot trust;
a dungless world is one their praise avoids.

35

Dressed all in black, a solitary crow
keeps his low office near the peacock cage.
Odd juxtapose.
               Exotics shriek their rage
and strut themselves through blue-green stridulence
while he sits hunched behind a rusty fence
where people never stop to mutter *Oh*!
Far overhead, the wild crows come and go.

36

On cindered pathways of the zoo
the children surge through April noon
breaking their silver laughter with
quick punctuations of balloon

while boats in hesitance explore
the sculptured contours of lagoon
obey the subtle thrust of Time
and float through plastic Now to Soon.

37

Made signal by the aphrodisiac
which doubly crowns their snouts, rhinoceri
stand wattled in thick skin, plaque over plaque,
which harbors them against the glaring sky,

or keeps them merely from the puzzled fly
which tastes a porcine smell but misses blood
since that deep joy flows hidden under mud
and, under that, the iron depth of skin
which foiled mouths bred in Tertiary slime.

Their hot hot hearts sustain an antique rhyme.

Meanwhile in Asia where the myth holds good
and hopeful geldings gorge on doctored food,
the silent poachers watch the jungle trails,
pursue the beast, pursue, and still pursue.

Within a bursting shade, green, hot, and full,
the bullets strike, a sinewed pattern fails,
the horns are savaged from the broken skull,
an ageless strength dissolves to stinking grue.

38

While bird buffoons who love a noisy town
of cockateels, macaws, and parrots lurch
along their birdlime boughs to upside-down
the screech owl stiffens back upon its perch:

its feathers sleek its body, tight and tight;
it looks out through the puzzle of its cage,
and memories that map the fields of night
shake its whole being with electric rage.

39

As coarse as muskeg or the northern wind,
or not unlike an Irish elk, the moose
bears massive beams that sweep a palmate span;
his bearded bell swings heavily and loose;
his humping shoulders ride on iron bones;
his narrow haunches prove a folklore lust;
his great split hoof upsets the yellow stones
which pave his kingdom in the paddock plan
and wears them slowly down to sifting dust.

He rules where waterlilies cannot grow.

Despite his brawn, he's named with that swift clan
called caribou, whitetail, marsh deer, and roe.

40

Some ecologic facts are gently true.

Star-nosed or common, always velvet-skinned,
the mole lives deep beneath the softest wind,
denies display, and loves obscurity:
no bars hold him to any fealty.

He has apartments underneath the zoo.

41

Behind thin sheets of frightened glass,
in crazy glooms of infra-red,
the clustered vampire bats suspend
from ragged branches that portend
the final attitude of dread,
the broken stiffness of the dead;

and humans peering through that glass
where vampires clutch at murdered trees
can peer into a sullen home,
know Transylvania has come,
and learn how blood shall slow and freeze
despite the heart's exigencies.

42

As straight as linchpins but more subtly taut,
the prairie dogs sit upright in a town
they were not let to make.

                   All undistraught,
and grown immune to any passing clown
who aims imaginary guns, they seem
like illustrations from a children's book:
See! Here's the rodent in the rodent's dream!

Not so.
            The prairie dogs are real.

                      They look
alertly at the children passing by,
and brightness matches brightness in each eye
as blue eyes look at brown or brown at brown.

The prairie dogs sit upright in their town.

43

With an entire and quiet lust, that
sensualist, the brown Himalayan cat
(but also striped and vaguely Bengalese)
should loll like muscled liquid in the sun

or crouch in steelspring ecstasy before
some flowered jungle floor
where fat hares run.

44

An easy springe to catch Lamarckians
or those who think the world was surely made
in one simplistic orgy of God's will,
this voiceless head, this dreaming eminence
moves high above a painted iron fence

or looms amid the maple sapling shade
which dies along the dapple of its skin.

Its horns are merest spikes, knobby and dull,
its tail inconsequential, briefly thin.

Serene beyond the nibbling reach of sin,
the tall giraffe possesses bones that spill
in elongated order from its skull
down to splaying hooves:

                                nevertheless,
held up by subtle strings of nothingness,
it seems to walk from the sky,
not subject to the earth or gravity.

Of all the myriad that throngs the zoo,
it is,

        if unbelieved,

                        the creature who
can demonstrate for children what God sees
as He dreams forth a world that is adorned
(as April worlds should be) with gentleness —
and magic worked beyond its last degrees.

45

(For Anne)

In jungle mode and tawny sarabande,
five lions move across the moated sand:

their roars invade the soft precincts of air;
their bodies lend the earth a golden hue;
their litheness hurls through flashings when they run;
mere presence sets their seal upon the zoo.

The far, refulgent fires of the sun
descend the gyring reaches of the sky
to forge a union with this ambience:
all things assume an Afric guise thereby.

An oak tree turns to thornbush;
                              Kenya lies
extended through the zoo in radiance,
a frame for splendor;
                              humans, in surprise,
watch majesty leap forth from its disguise.

Five lions moving in the supple sun
hold Africa enorbed in their great eyes.

Power, of course, but after power, pride,
and after that, a grace that rules the pride.

46

Unlike the seals that own a larger lake,
though hardly happier, the otters thrive
within a silver pool;
                              sweet clowns, they make
the April magic deeper;
                              their lithe forms
divide the frolic waters with the spark
of sunlight tossed through sunlight;
                                        their eyes mark
a death for any shadow;
                              they contrive
kaleidoscopes from lissome joy;
                                    they dive
through antic swirls as if their hearts must raise
the world to matching joy, warmblooded, bright.

Then here see water, flesh, and fire glance
upon and through each other:
                                    such acts praise
a God who swims through all evolving worlds
as He creates them out of death and night.

The Paraclete sustains the otter dance
and all the dances in the spheres of light.

The eft is orange but the newt is green:
this miracle occurs outside the zoo.